DATE DUE

Other Books of Related Interest in the Opposing Viewpoints Series:

Biomedical Ethics
Civil Liberties
Constructing a Life Philosophy
Death and Dying
The Environmental Crisis

Additional Books in the Opposing Viewpoints Series:

Abortion
AIDS
American Foreign Policy
American Government
The American Military
American Values
America's Elections
America's Prisons
The Arms Race
Censorship
Central America
Chemical Dependency
Crime & Criminals
Criminal Justice
The Death Penalty
Drug Abuse
Economics in America
Latin America and U.S. Foreign Policy
Male/Female Roles
The Mass Media
The Middle East
Nuclear War
The Political Spectrum
Poverty
Problems of Africa
Sexual Values
Social Justice
The Soviet Union
Teenage Sexuality
Terrorism
The Vietnam War
War and Human Nature